89th
U. S. Open

Oak Hill

Writer
Gary Nuhn

Photographer
Lawrence Levy

Editor
Bev Norwood

Assistant Editor
Jan Davis

ISBN 0-9615344-7-8

©1989 United States Golf Association®
Golf House, Far Hills, New Jersey 07931

Statistics produced by Unisys Corporation

Published by International Merchandising Corporation,
One Erieview Plaza, Cleveland, Ohio 44114

Printed in the United States of America

89th U.S. Open

Official Annual Presented by

ROLEX

As is their custom, my friends at Rolex were host to a dinner on the evening before the U.S. Open at Rochester. It was my pleasure to be there and to be introduced by the defending champion, Curtis Strange. We both talked for a while about what it meant to be the champion, and how Curtis and I had compared our recollections after his victory in 1988.

To win the U.S. Open once can be the highlight of a player's career. To win twice, especially twice in a row, is truly a great achievement. Congratulations again, Curtis.

This annual book, sponsored for the fifth year by Rolex, presents the story in words and photographs of the 1989 U.S. Open. Proceeds from sales through the USGA Associates Program will benefit junior golf. I recommend it to you.

Arnold Palmer

89th U.S. Open

June 15-18, 1989, Oak Hill Country Club, Rochester, New York

Contestant	Rounds				Total	Prize
Curtis Strange	71	64	73	70	278	$200,000.00
Ian Woosnam	70	68	73	68	279	67,823.00
Mark McCumber	70	68	72	69	279	67,823.00
Chip Beck	71	69	71	68	279	67,823.00
Brian Claar	71	72	68	69	280	34,345.00
Masashi Ozaki	70	71	68	72	281	28,220.50
Scott Simpson	67	70	69	75	281	28,220.50
Peter Jacobsen	71	70	71	70	282	24,307.00
Jose-Maria Olazabal	69	72	70	72	283	19,968.50
Hubert Green	69	72	74	68	283	19,968.50
Tom Kite	67	69	69	78	283	19,968.50
Paul Azinger	71	72	70	70	283	19,968.50
Tom Pernice Jr.	67	75	68	74	284	15,634.20
Mark Lye	71	69	72	72	284	15,634.20
Scott Hoch	70	72	70	72	284	15,634.20
Larry Nelson	68	73	68	75	284	15,634.20
Payne Stewart	66	75	72	71	284	15,634.20
Nick Faldo	68	72	73	72	285	13,013.00
David Frost	73	72	70	70	285	13,013.00
Jay Don Blake	66	71	72	76	285	13,013.00
Steve Elkington	70	70	78	68	286	11,306.00
Nolan Henke	75	69	72	70	286	11,306.00
D.A. Weibring	70	74	73	69	286	11,306.00
Fred Couples	74	71	67	74	286	11,306.00
Bill Glasson	73	70	70	73	286	11,306.00
Ray Floyd	68	74	74	71	287	9,983.67
Don Pooley	74	69	71	73	287	9,983.67
Robert Wrenn	74	71	73	69	287	9,983.66
Hal Sutton	69	75	72	72	288	9,006.50
Scott Allen Taylor	69	71	76	72	288	9,006.50
Emlyn Aubrey	69	73	73	73	288	9,006.50
Dan Pohl	71	71	73	73	288	9,006.50
Dan Forsman	70	70	76	73	289	7,576.60
Mark Wiebe	69	71	72	77	289	7,576.60
Brad Faxon	73	70	75	71	289	7,576.60
Greg Norman	72	68	73	76	289	7,576.60
Isao Aoki	70	70	75	74	289	7,576.60
Edward Kirby	70	70	73	76	289	7,576.60
Davis Love III	71	74	73	71	289	7,576.60
Larry Mize	72	72	71	74	289	7,576.60
Joey Sindelar	67	77	74	71	289	7,576.60
Billy Mayfair	72	69	76	72	289	7,576.60
Jack Nicklaus	67	74	74	75	290	6,281.00
Seve Ballesteros	75	70	76	69	290	6,281.00
Clark Dennis	72	72	72	74	290	6,281.00
Ken Green	73	72	71	75	291	5,485.80
Tom Watson	76	69	73	73	291	5,485.80
John Mahaffey	77	68	74	72	291	5,485.80

Contestant		Rounds			Total	Prize
Richard Zokol	71	69	76	75	291	5,485.80
Steve Jones	69	75	77	70	291	5,485.80
Tom Sieckmann	73	71	74	74	292	4,690.00
Steve Pate	74	69	73	76	292	4,690.00
Jodie Mudd	73	71	74	74	292	4,690.00
Webb Heintzelman	72	70	75	76	293	4,299.80
Ronnie Black	71	74	76	72	293	4,299.80
David Ogrin	73	72	73	75	293	4,299.80
Hale Irwin	74	70	79	70	293	4,299.80
Chris Perry	76	67	72	78	293	4,299.80
Clarence Rose	70	75	73	76	294	4,120.00
Bernhard Langer	66	78	77	73	294	4,120.00
David Graham	73	72	77	73	295	4,099.00
Mark Calcavecchia	74	70	74	77	295	4,099.00
Tony Sills	72	72	71	81	296	4,099.00
* Gregory Lesher	70	72	76	78	296	Medal
Dan Haldorson	72	70	76	78	296	4,099.00
Bobby Wadkins	73	72	75	77	297	4,099.00
Dillard Pruitt	68	74	81	75	298	4,099.00
Ed Humenik	73	72	76	77	298	4,099.00
Doug Weaver	72	73	80	75	300	4,099.00
John Daly	74	67	80	79	300	4,099.00
Kurt Beck	68	73	83	77	301	4,099.00

Bill Buttner 71-75—146
Dave Eichelberger 73-73—146
Nick Price 74-72—146
Lanny Wadkins 73-73—146
Ben Crenshaw 73-73—146
Bob Mann 72-74—146
Dennis Trixler 73-73—146
Bob Gilder 71-75—146
Mac O'Grady 73-73—146
Jeff Sluman 75-71—146
Jim Hallet 73-73—146
John Adams 71-75—146
Leonard Thompson 75-71—146
Bob Proben 73-73—146
John Huston 73-74—147
Loren Roberts 72-75—147
Mike Reid 72-75—147
Gary Player 78-69—147
Fred Funk 72-75—147
Steven Bowman 76-71—147
Andy North 72-75—147
Jay Haas 69-78—147
David Edwards 74-73—147
Bill Sander 72-75—147
Jim Carter 73-74—147
Mark McNulty 73-74—147
Roger Gunn 71-76—147
Ken Schall 72-76—148
Jerry Pate 74-74—148

Bob Tway 74-74—148
Jack Ferenz 70-78—148
Stan Utley 74-74—148
Tim Simpson 74-74—148
Gordon J. Brand 76-72—148
Bill Britton 71-78—149
Steve Lamontagne 78-71—149
Jim Gallagher Jr. 74-75—149
Wayne Grady 75-74—149
Keith Clearwater 74-76—150
*Eric Meeks 75-75—150
Ed Fiori 73-77—150
Denny Hepler 77-73—150
Tommy Armour III 74-77—151
Duffy Waldorf 78-73—151
John Mazza 80-71—151
Dan Oschmann 77-74—151
Fuzzy Zoeller 78-73—151
Jim Booros 75-76—151
Brian Tennyson 75-76—151
Mark O'Meara 78-73—151
*Greg Reid 76-76—152
Danny Mijovic 76-76—152
P.H. Horgan III 77-75—152
Sandy Lyle 78-74—152
Michael Burke Jr. 77-75—152
Jim Roy 77-75—152
James McGovern 79-73—152
Michael Brisky 76-76—152

John Burckle 80-72—152
Brian Fogt 77-75—152
*Jay Sigel 77-76—153
Michael Walton 79-74—153
*Eric Hogg 74-79—153
Andy Bean 70-83—153
Lee Trevino 74-79—153
Mike Donald 80-73—153
Steve Hart 74-80—154
Steve Schroeder 79-75—154
Buddy Gardner 76-78—154
Martin Schiene 77-77—154
Ken Krieger 76-78—154
Gary Koch 74-81—155
Paul Oglesby 77-79—156
Scott Williams 81-75—156
Don Reese 76-80—156
David Glenz 79-77—156
Jeff Fairfield 78-79—157
Kevin Healy 76-82—158
John Fleischer 76-82—158
Rick Flesher 76-83—159
Jeffrey Bloom 81-80—161
Jon Fiedler 77-84—161
Greg Chapman 78-84—162
*Jonathon Yarian 90-88—178
Gil Morgan 71 WD

Professionals not returning 72-hole scores received $1,000 each.

*Denotes amateur.

5

89th
U. S. Open
Oak Hill

You look at it now, with these magnificent stands of trees — trees as far as one can see in every direction — and it is difficult, nearly impossible, to imagine what it must have been like in the 1920s when the original members of Oak Hill Country Club agreed to move here.

George Eastman of the Eastman Kodak Eastmans was riding in one of those new-fangled aeroplanes in 1922 when he saw the old Oak Hill (built in 1901) and decided it was a perfect location.

The catch: he thought it perfect for a university, not a golf course.

Eastman convinced the membership to sell him that property, upon which the University of Rochester now sits, and in return he provided them a new site.

This site.

Historians tell us how barren it was. Just farmland with some fences. Three hundred fifty-five acres of dirt, and not particularly good dirt at that. It wasn't exactly the surface of the moon, but it wasn't too many steps removed.

What dreams those men must have had to have finished with this — two gorgeous golf courses; the mandatory, stately English Tudor clubhouse covered by ivy; and what did I read somewhere, 40,000 oak trees? Forty thousand?

The mind boggles.

Donald Ross designed and built the two original courses in 1926. Robert Trent Jones was hired to add muscle to the East Course before the 1956 Open. Jones retouched the East again before the 1968 Open. Finally, yet another member of golf's architectural fra-

Hole No. 14, a 323-yard par 4 known as Bunker Hill, played to a 4.08 average.

7

ternity, George Fazio, authored another facelift before the 1980 PGA.

Which of the three had the most profound effect on the East Course and on the 1989 Open?

None of them.

Dr. John R. Williams did.

Williams was a research physician whose life's work deserves more than a couple of paragraphs in a golf book. He was in the forefront of the push for refrigerators in every house. He pioneered the use of insulin to treat diabetes. He founded a hospital.

He put the oaks in Oak Hill.

Yes, it pales in comparison to his work in refrigeration and insulin, but John R. Williams' work at Oak Hill came from the same place in his being. Williams couldn't do anything halfway. Once he was involved in something, it was not all-or-nothing, it was just "all."

Named chairman of the landscaping committee, Williams was surrounded by men who made their living doing this. He thus bowed to their expertise at first. But when the first planting of 6,000 shrubs withered in the Rochester summer, Williams decided to take a more hands-on approach. He began collecting seedlings and planting them in his own backyard. When they were established enough, he would transplant them to the golf course. Tedious? Yes. Effective? Judge the results. Most of the trees at Oak Hill spent their childhood in John R. Williams' backyard.

The golf world discovered Oak Hill in

Photo: Oak Hill Country Club/Sports Marketing Group Inc.

Dr. John R. Williams put the oaks in Oak Hill.

1949 when the USGA brought the U.S. Amateur championship here. Charlie Coe won it. The membership then bid for and won the 1956 Open. It would be Oak Hill's "coming out party" at the grand old age of 30. The members were worried the world's best pros would devour their beloved, so they hired Jones, a Rochester native, to make her less palatable. He took his charge seriously. Jones changed 17 holes, including construction of seven new tees and 26 new bunkers. He added 364 yards, rebuilt 27 bunkers and added mounds and knolls.

At least one of the world's finest wasn't impressed. Ben Hogan called Oak Hill "the easiest I've ever seen for a National Open."

A week later, Hogan had probably changed his mind. No man broke par. Cary Middlecoff came closest. His one-over 281 beat Hogan and Julius Boros by one.

The finish was textbook Open. Middlecoff, a chain-smoking, nerve-twitching Tennessean who played golf on the jagged edge, took the lead in the 36-hole final round with a morning 70 and was sculpting a runaway as he approached the final three holes in the afternoon. Runaway begone. He bogeyed 16 and 17 and was just about to bogey 18 when he composed himself for one final magnificent chip to four feet to save par.

Three men had a chance to tie, but the Open pressure, or aura, or whatever you choose to call it, was too much. Hogan needed three pars on the final three holes. He got one at 16, but at 17, with a three-footer to save par, he set himself over it, stared into the depths of golf's soul and stepped away. It was a stunning moment — perhaps the greatest golfer up to that time faced down by a ball, a cup and three feet of real estate. He quickly readdressed, stabbed and missed.

The other two finishes weren't nearly as Shakespearean. Boros needed one birdie in the last four holes to tie. He hit masterful shots and burned the cup three times, but there is no place on the scorecard for burned cups. Like Hogan, Ted Kroll needed three pars to tie. But he hooked his tee ball on 16 into a spruce, made triple bogey and became a footnote.

That Open was such a success, the USGA awarded its crown jewel to Oak Hill again in 1968. Jones made one more change, but it was striking. He built a new hole, a par-three that became the fifth, in order to facilitate crowd traffic in the middle of the course.

Lee Trevino returned to the site of his 1968 win.

It was that Open, the Lee Trevino Open, that became one of golf's landmarks — the day The Big Three (Arnie, Jack and Gary) finally broke apart not just in reality but in golf fans' minds. The actual breakup had come years before with the rise to prominence of Billy Casper. But when this unknown, this Lee Trevino fellow, won the Open and continued to pile up victories across the breadth of the PGA Tour, it was only then that "The Big Three" left golf's lexicon.

Trevino's victory wasn't a thing of beauty. No one dressed like *that* with a swing like *that* could produce anything resembling a

rose. What he did, however, was win convincingly, which in golf equates with beauty. He won by four shots, which is like winning the Super Bowl by four touchdowns. And when it was over, most of us forgave him the socks that looked as if he'd dunked them in Red Dye No. 2, and the Band Aid on his arm. And, yes, the way he stalked his putts like a cowboy circling a rattlesnake.

Trevino was basically anonymous even though he had finished fifth in the previous Open and had a pair of second-place finishes on the regular tour earlier that season. He was so anonymous that even after shooting 69-68 in the first two rounds, he could sit in a golf cart near the pro shop sipping beer and not be bothered by anyone for an autograph. "I think they thought I was the cart guy or something," Trevino said.

He added another 69 on Saturday and went to the final round one shot behind onetime West Point cadet Bert Yancey. The nearest other warm body, Jack Nicklaus, was seven shots back. Yancey and Trevino both started poorly, but Trevino recovered and Yancey didn't. Trevino, leading by one, birdied 11 and 12, and Yancey bogeyed 13. Ball game. The Man in the Red Socks parred in to tie Nicklaus's Open record of 275 and, with his final-round 68, became the first man in Open history to shoot four rounds under 70.

Oak Hill's leaders wanted another Open, but couldn't pin one down. The consensus among them was the course was being perceived as too easy. In 1974, they hired yet another architect to put a bit of a beast into the East.

Enter the Fazios, George and Tom.

Enter a fury of protest.

Whereas Jones had pretty much stayed with the original Donald Ross design, the Fazios made wholesale changes, including four totally new greens, a pond at the 15th and the redesign of what many considered Oak Hill's finest hole, the sixth.

The club immediately landed the 1980 PGA championship and although many of the pros complained about the changes, they played. Nicklaus, one of the most critical, won with a six-under 274, but he was the only man under par. Andy Bean was second at one-over 281.

The USGA was apparently impressed. It awarded the 1989 Open to Oak Hill. While waiting, Oak Hill was host to the 1984 Sen-

ior Open, won by Miller Barber.

For this Open, the East Course was left pretty much intact. The 13th was lengthened from 565 yards to 594. The 15th green was redone so tee shots near the water didn't automatically get wet.

So when the pros arrived the week of June 11, they found an amalgam of Donald Ross, Robert Trent Jones and the Fazios to play on. And they would walk in the footsteps of Charlie Coe, Cary Middlecoff, Lee Trevino, Jack Nicklaus and Miller Barber. But mostly they found the product of a research physician's passion and persistence. The Open and the course wouldn't have happened without Dr. John R. Williams and his 40,000 seedlings.

Old friends and rivals, Jack Nicklaus and Lee Trevino, were reunited in the U.S. Open.

Only 39 birdies were posted as No. 18, 440 yards and par 4, played to a 4.30 average.

The new verb of the pre-championship festivities: "Squeegeed." Used in a sentence: "A member of the grounds crew squeegeed water off the fairway with a rubber rolling device, then squeegeed it again, then squeegeed it again, then stood and watched water seep up out of the ground and reform a puddle the size of Rhode Island."

This is another way of saying Rochester was wet when the lads arrived. It had rained throughout the spring. Maybe rained isn't strong enough. It had rained, drizzled, sprinkled, teemed, poured, stormed and then, just for kicks, it went through the cycle again . . . and again. . . and . . .

The prediction was peachy, too.

Monday: Heavy rains at night.

Tuesday: Forty percent chance of showers and thunderstorms.

Wednesday: Sixty percent chance of showers.

Thursday: Rain likely.

Friday: Scattered showers.

Saturday: Scattered showers.

Oak Hill? Hah! Soak Hill.

Eventually, P.J. Boatwright, USGA executive director of rules and competitions, would say it was "the worst string of days we've ever had ... I've never seen a course as damaged as this one."

But wait. The literature probably warned us of this, didn't it?

Let's take a look at "A visitor's guide to Rochester."

• "Architecture in Rochester is especially noteworthy," it says. (OK, but what about the weather?)

Oak Hill became Soak Hill for the U. S. Open week in Rochester.

• "Rochester can claim more buildings in the National Register of Historic Places than any other city its size," it says. (OK, but what about the weather?)

• "A short drive out of the city is the Finger Lakes area," it says. (OK, but what about the weather?)

Let Andy Bean tell you about the weather: "We'll be out there tomorrow with our boots and boats," he said Wednesday.

And Jim Booros: "My caddy told me we have a 9:11 tee time," Booros said. "I told him, 'Shoot, by 9:30, we'll be calling 911.'"

And Brian Fogt: "You can barely walk out there it's so soft."

And let Lee Trevino tell you about it after he asked for the forecast and was told more rain, "Man, it's already so wet I can't reach the par-threes."

Boatwright said, "I don't know about the draining capabilities of the course, but with as much rain as we've had this spring, if we get a heavy shower, we'd be out of business."

The heavy shower hit at noon Wednesday and lasted on into the night. It would turn out that only the near-perfect condition of the course plus yeoman work by Oak Hill superintendent Joe Hahn and his staff would keep the tournament from floating away later in the week.

The weather was one of the main themes of the pre-tournament palaver, but there were numerous others, among them:

• Curtis Strange's quest to become the first repeat champion since Ben Hogan in 1951.

• Seve Ballesteros' effort to win his first U.S. Open, despite a restricted American schedule.

• Lee Trevino's attempt, 21 years later, to rediscover that magic elixir of youth, not to mention another four-leaf clover.

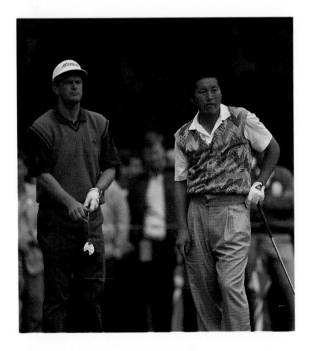

Sandy Lyle (left) was a favorite, while Jumbo Ozaki was not so well-regarded.

• Homeboy Jeff Sluman's local knowledge and why he was passing it on to Greg Norman.

• Did ESPN's Chris Berman slander Rochester or didn't he? (He didn't.)

Strange's attempted repeat, although it received the requisite attention, was not taken seriously by many, if only because men just don't win the Open back-to-back anymore. They used to, sure. But they don't anymore.

Why? Well, uh ... just because.

Strange was tip-toeing through the repeat talk. "My game suits up well for an Open course," he said. "But that's as far as I go. I don't want to put my foot in my mouth. You don't win Opens on Thursday and Friday. I mean, you have to be patient. I just want to be in striking distance for Saturday and Sunday."

Prescient words, it would turn out.

Spain's Seve Ballesteros, the reigning British Open champion (opposite).

England's Nick Faldo, 1989 Masters champion and runner-up in the 1988 U.S. Open.

The new verb of the day: "Pubgolf."

Used in a sentence: "It was so wet, it was like throwing darts at the green. It reminded me of World War II, when I was in London, saving democracy as we know it and also having an ale or two in an English pub. Hey I know. These guys pubgolfed their balls today."

The day dawned gray and got grayer. The sky looked like a massive herd of elephants ... in gray sweaters with black trim. The air was so thick, you didn't so much walk through it as you waded, swam, even fought through it, like a man with a machete in the deepest Amazon jungle.

But, with a couple of brief exceptions, the rain, which always seemed just 30 seconds in the future, somehow stayed away. With the already-saturated course ready to surrender to any good downpour, Someone Up There gave the Open a reprieve. Apparently, Some-one Up There is a golf fan, the difference being He doesn't have to stand in line to catch a bus back to the parking lot.

The morning scoreboard belonged to Emlyn Aubrey. When that name went up, one had to assume this was the latest foreign invasion, perhaps some unknown from Ireland. "Who's he?" looks scrunched up spectators' faces. Books rippled in the press tent. The books didn't mention Ireland. "Grew up in Reading, Pennsylvania," they said. "1986 graduate of LSU."

Emlyn Aubrey? This year's Lee Trevino?

Aubrey made the turn at one-over-par, then birdied 10, 11, 13 and 15. He was three-under-par and leading the Open. Then he double-bogeyed 17.

"Emlyn Aubrey just remembered where he was," someone said. It's a realization that strikes many men at the Open, not just relative unknowns. You're cruisin'. You look at the leaderboard and see your name. You crash. A-B-C.

What the early leg of Emlyn Aubrey was showing was that the course was defenseless. Oak Hill was Bambi wandering lost on the first day of deer-hunting season. A wet course may haunt average players, but it's a blessing to pros. They hit the ball and it stays where they hit it. No worries about bad rolls or bad bounces; only bad karma. They play darts as if in an English pub.

So the leaderboard was splashed in red, like the scenery in a Rambo movie. Eventually, 21 men would break par, an Open first-round record.

Aubrey having backed off slightly, the midday leaderboard belonged to Bernhard Langer, the man with the world's — or at least the Open's — strangest putting stroke. To even attempt to describe it is to risk reader revolt.

I'll risk it. First, Langer puts his left hand on the putter with the back of his hand facing the hole. The grip of the putter extends several inches up the inside of his forearm.

Wait. It gets better.

He takes his right hand and grabs hold of his left wrist, pinning the top of the putter handle. The man then putts one-handed back-handed, the way you might chase away a fly at a picnic. Bret Maverick had an ace up his sleeve; Houdini had the key to the handcuffs; Bernhard Langer has a putter.

Langer's goal is to keep his hands and wrists completely out of the stroke; to make the stroke all arms; to "pendulum" the doggone ball (yet another neo-verb invented before your eyes).

The idea worked Thursday. The West

After his 66, Payne Stewart said, "I'm making the four-to-six footers that keep a round going."

German fired eight birdies — "I didn't think there were eight birdies out there," he said — and signed for a four-under-par 66. His back-nine was Adventure Golf. He made one par. By definition, that makes the par the big news. It came at 17 (driver, 6-iron to the fringe, two putts). On the other eight holes, he had four birdies and four bogeys, so the scales of golf, like the scales of jus-tice, were evenly bal-anced. His best stretch was 14, 15 and 16 (birdies every one). But a final three-putt bogey at 18 cost him the outright lead.

The leader door thus open, two oth-ers hurried through — Payne Stewart and Jay Don Blake.

Stewart, the NFL's favorite pro, was wearing his New York Jets outfit, and he was as good as the Jets are bad. His irons were leaving craters near the holes — 6-iron to a foot-and-a-half at No. 1; 7-iron to three feet at No. 8; 9-iron to one foot at No. 12. When he bogeyed 15 and 16, it didn't faze him. He birdied 17 and 18 to get the lost shots right back.

Then Mr. Knickers told about the rest of his week's sartorial plans: Buffalo Bills on Friday; New York Giants on Saturday; Cincinnati Bengals on Sunday.

"Why?" someone asked.

"Because that's how they were stacked in my suitcase," Stewart said.

Blake soon made it a triumvirate at 66, surviving a double bogey at No. 5 when he couldn't convince officials to allow him relief from a "squishy lie" in the rough where spectator traffic had matted the grass. He chunked that shot to lead to the double. Some men burn through shirt collars after that kind of incident. Blake burned the course, instead, with consecutive birdies at six, seven and eight.

Jay Don Blake survived a double bogey at No. 5.

Eventually, he slid in a 16-foot birdie at 18 for his 66, then told about a time when his pro career was on serious hold — 1984 and 1985, when he went home to St. George, Utah, and worked in a hardware store. "I was pretty discouraged," he said. "I felt I had a good enough game to be out here. It was pretty hard to deal with the fact I wasn't."

Late in the day — in the gloom — Hal Sutton briefly teased the leaders by climbing to four-under. But he went for a double bogey on 16 to leave all the writers' early stories intact.

The group at 67 was, like the leader group, mostly Establishment — Jack Nicklaus, Scott Simpson, Tom Kite, Joey Sindelar — with a single interloper, Tom Pernice.

Pernice, a 29-year-old fourth-year tour pro from Lees Summit, Missouri, was perfect casting. You can't have an Open without a Tom Pernice high on the leaderboard after one round. The name changes every year, but the mystery doesn't. Pernice turned at one-over-par and shot a cute, little 31 on the back, birdieing all the even-numbered holes except 18.

"Are you surprised," someone asked, "that at some point late in the round you didn't say, 'Hey, this is the Open. What am I doin' here?'"

"Not at all," he said. "I feel like I've been out here long enough that I understand the golf swing. I feel like I belong out here."

He said this despite having finished 148th, 195th and 150th on the money list his first three years and sitting 215th for this year as

"I didn't think there were eight birdies out there," said Bernhard Langer (opposite), but the German star found them.

he spoke. But if he didn't say that—if he didn't believe he belonged — he might as well pack it up and go back to Lees Summit.

Ironically, Pernice's best previous tournament was last year's Texas Open, where he

First Round

Bernhard Langer	66
Payne Stewart	66
Jay Don Blake	66
Scott Simpson	67
Jack Nicklaus	67
Tom Kite	67
Joey Sindelar	67
Tom Pernice, Jr.	67

finished tie-fifth. The name of the course in San Antonio? Oak Hills.

Of the four other 67s, Nicklaus's made the most noise. Here he was at age 49 trying for his fifth Open title. He credited his score to rediscovering positive thinking. "The last few years," he said, "I've stood on the tee

Even at age 49, Jack Nicklaus (opposite) had plenty of reason to smile in the first round.

Although he surprised most, Tom Pernice felt he belonged at the top.

Seve Ballesteros and Curtis Strange decide the nearest point of relief after Ballesteros' shot hit the bridge and went in the water at No. 5. He took double bogey en route to a 75.

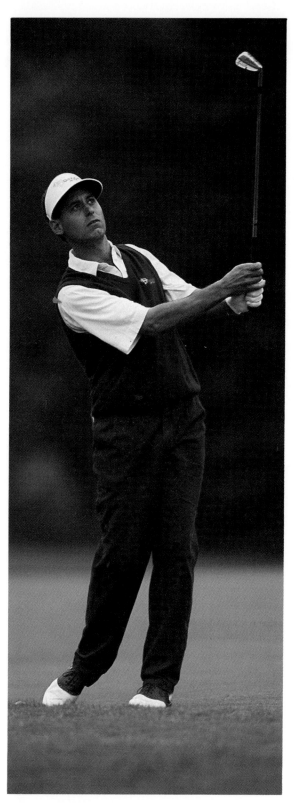

Beck — Kurt, not Chip (unrelated) — was among the first-round leaders.

thinking, 'Where is the best place to miss it?' Or, 'How do I avoid this situation?' Today I tried to think where I wanted the ball to go instead of where I didn't want it to go."

It went in a fairway bunker on No. 1 to cost him his only bogey. After that he birdied two, six, 10 and 13, made a couple of dandy saves and generally comported himself as the Jack of Old.

Nicklaus was also involved in two of Thursday's best press tent exchanges.

"Has the rain moderated the peril of the course?" someone asked.

"Moderated the apparel?" Nicklaus said quizzically.

"No, moderated the peril," the man tried again.

"Anytime it rains," Nicklaus said, "it modifies the peril of a golf course. It modifies your apparel, too."

Still sharp of club, still sharp of tongue.

Someone else said, "You look more robust."

"Robust is fat," Jack countered.

"That's the question," the man said.

All laughed, including the object of the skewer.

"I'm maybe 193-94-95," Jack said. "Maybe 10 pounds heavier than I'd like to be. But only two, three pounds heavier than I've been the last couple of years." So yes, but no. Got it?

The 67 tied Jack's best round in an Open since his opening 63 at Baltusrol in 1980 (he also shot 67 in the third round at Shinnecock in 1986). It also brought up the question, "Can a 49-year-old geezer win the Open?"

"I don't know," Nicklaus said, "but I'm either gullible enough or dumb enough to believe I can do what I did today for three more days."

Few others were ready to rule him out, either.

Simpson, the 1986 Open champion, had the best reply when asked if Nicklaus could keep it up. "If he doesn't get nervous with the pressure, he can," Simpson said.

From the "Oh, By The Way" file: The defending champion, Curtis Strange—remember him? — made double bogey at 17 and shot one-over-par 71. I mean, just in case someone thinks it might be important.

Hometown favorite and PGA champion Jeff Sluman (opposite) was in trouble with his opening 75. He missed the 36-hole cut.

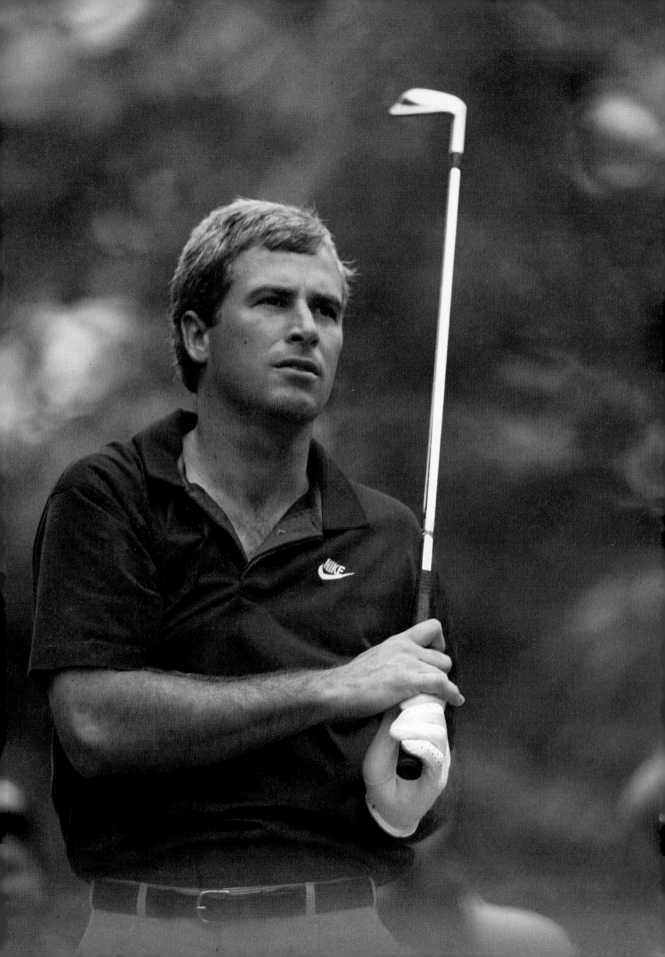

The new verb of the day: "Strange." Also the noun of the day and the adjective.

Used in a sentence: "It was a strange, weird, bizarre day, and it was also a Curtis Strange day and if it got any stranger, it would have stranged credibility."

Came Friday morning and came the most amazing string of shots in U.S. Open history ... maybe in golf history. By 10:05 a.m., there already had been four holes-in-one.

More amazing: All four aces were on the 167-yard sixth.

Most amazing: The world didn't come to an end.

Oh, yes, in general, holes-in-one are meaningless. Some terrific players never smell one. Yet grandmothers make them. And 10-year-olds make them. And first-time players make them.

What they don't do is make them back-to-back-to-back-to-back. In less than two hours. On the same hole. With the same club (7-iron). With the crowd and the marshals dancing like Greeks at a wedding reception.

Here's how this magical, mystical tour went (all times EDT and approximate):

• 8:15: Doug Weaver, member of the day's first group, draws a 7-iron out of his bag, nails it 10 feet past and to the right of the cup and the ball, as if on a yo-yo string, sucks back into the hole.

• 9:25: Seven groups later. Mark Wiebe draws a 7-iron out of his bag, hits a shot so similar to Weaver's it could be an instant replay (except TV cameras didn't catch any of these), and it sucks back into the hole too.

Curtis Strange's 64 tied Ben Hogan's course record and was one stroke off the U.S. Open record.

• 9:50: Two groups later. Jerry Pate draws a 7-iron out of his bag. Ditto. Know what I mean?

• 10:05: The very next group. Nick Price draws a 7-iron out of his bag and ... oh, never mind. It's in. That's all you need to know.

That was four bullseyes in the first 33 players. Not only had there never been anything like it in the Open, there had never been anything like it in real life, either.

Golf Digest said the odds against a pro scoring a single ace were 3,708 to 1. Using that number and the law of probability, a University of Rochester mathematician calculated the odds as 10 million to 1. ESPN quoted a Harvard professor as saying the odds were 415 quintillion to 1 (a quintillion, he said, has 15 zeros).

Writers on the case were less zero-crazy. Myself, for instance, I figured it this way: This is the 89th Open; it's happened once; the odds are therefore 89 to 1. Just call me Mr. Math.

Later the Four Aces, as they quickly became known, gathered for a group picture, then matched war stories.

Weaver and Price each listed the yardage at 159. Wiebe and Pate each said it was 160. That should give you an idea of how imprecise this hole-in-one science is.

Said Weaver, "It was like lightning hit."

Said Wiebe, "It was just one of those fluky deals."

Said Pate, "As soon as it left my club I knew it was in. Then I heard a scream from the green, and I knew it was my wife. She's a screamer."

Said Price, "It was the strangest thing I've ever seen or been a part of."

Wiebe got to thinking with all those other players still out there, someone else just might make it five.

"No," said USGA director of communications John Morris, "there won't be any more.

We've planted a tree on that green."

With the course abuzz about the aces, the defending champion started to sneak up the leaderboard as the sun came out for the first time since Tuesday. Strange had been in good shape, one under par, until he double-bogeyed 17 Thursday. He recovered those two shots

Second Round

Curtis Strange	64-135
Tom Kite	69-136
Scott Simpson	70-137
Jay Don Blake	71-137
Ian Woosnam	68-138
Mark McCumber	68-138

with 10-foot birdie putts on Nos. 1 and 2 Friday, then struck what for him has become "an Open tradition," as he called it — holing out a pitching wedge from 115 yards on No. 4 for an eagle.

Counting the four aces, it was the fifth full-swing hole-out of the day, and also Strange's fifth full-swing hole-out eagle in Opens — one at Winged Foot in 1984, two at Olympic in 1987 and one at The Country Club in 1988. Asked for an explanation, Strange said, "I don't

know. I guess you aim better at the Open."

His aim stayed true, even as the sun disappeared and several brief but powerful showers sped through, eventually causing standing water on several greens and a 14-minute cessation of play. None of this bothered Strange. The prematurely graying Virginian turned in 31, then smoothed a 5-iron to 20 feet at the 10th and made the putt to go five-under; hit a pitching wedge to 15 feet at the 14th and made it to go six-under; and dropped an 8-iron four feet away at the 16th and made it to go seven-under.

Seven-under is the Open record. Only Johnny Miller (1973 at Oakmont) and Jack Nicklaus and Tom Weiskopf (1980 at Baltusrol) had done it. "I wasn't even aware of it," Strange shrugged. "I was just tryin' to get in."

He didn't make it. As it had on Thursday, the 17th up and bit him again. He drove into the short rough, about two feet from where he had Thursday, then put his 4-wood into the same bunker as Thursday. This time, however, he hit a decent bunker shot to five feet (Thursday, he'd blasted across and off the green). Still, he missed the par-saver and his chance to tie

Ian Woosnam of Wales (opposite with his caddy), came in with a second-round 68.

Curtis Strange made four birdies and an eagle, but missed this record-equaling putt on the 18th green.

the all-time record went with it.

Asked if he was disappointed at not tying the record, Strange at first started to do a tongue-dance, pretending that shooting 63 would have made his life complete. But he abruptly stopped, smiled and said, "I could care less, to be honest with you. I was trying to B.S. you, but to tell you the truth, a 64 at Oak Hill ain't bad."

It, in fact, tied the competitive course record set in 1942 at a regular tour event by — irony of ironies — Ben Hogan. Those two names, Strange and Hogan, would be linked again before the weekend was over.

The six-under-par 64 gave Strange a two-day total of five-under 135 and a one-shot lead over Kite, who was 67-69—136. Blake (66-71) and Simpson (67-70) were another shot back at 137. Welshman Ian Woosnam, playing in his first Open, and Mark McCumber, one of America's most under-appreciated talents, were another shot back at 138, both having put up 70-68. Among 11 men looming at even-par 140, international superstars Nick Faldo and Greg

Tom Kite (opposite) struggled, but came in with 69 for second place.

A chip-in on No. 18 enabled Tom Watson to make the 36-hole cut.

A familiar position: Scott Simpson contending in the U.S. Open. He finished tied for sixth place.

Norman were ... well, the loomingest.

Not looming but sitting pretty at 142 was Greg Lesher of Lebanon, Pennsylvania, the only amateur (of six) to make the cut.

Has anyone seen Seve Ballesteros? You say he shot 75-70—145 and was right on the cut? Shake your head here. Every year. Every year we think this could be Seve's year. Every year it's not. Shake your head here.

While Strange was in full charge, some of Thursday's leaders were in full retreat. Langer went 66-78; Stewart 66-75; Nicklaus 67-74; Sindelar 67-77; Pernice 67-75. So much for preposterous putting styles; Buffalo Bills' outfits; positive thinking; remade swings (Sindelar); and first-round unknowns.

Perhaps the most important shot of the tournament for 14 players was Strange's 50-foot downhill putt on the 18th. He cozied it to about three inches from the cup and made par. Had he three-putted, he would have been at 136 and all 14 men at 146 would have stayed to play the final day under the "10-Stroke Rule."

As it was, those 14 and 70 others missed the cut.

Among the more noted victims were Nick Price, Lanny Wadkins, Ben Crenshaw and local favorite Sluman, all among the 146s; two-time Open champ Andy North (147); Fuzzy Zoeller (151); Sandy Lyle (152); and the Oak Hill-defender, Trevino (153).

The obvious question arose. No man has repeated as Open champion since Hogan — there's that name again – in 1950-51.

"It's too early to talk about that now," Strange said. "Let's talk about that Sunday."

But it would be difficult for him not to think about it Saturday because he would be paired with Kite, who just happens to have an equipment contract with the Hogan Co. And right there on Tom Kite's hat and shirt and various other pieces would be all the reminder Curtis Strange would need — the word "Hogan."

"I won't bring it up," Kite said, shrugging. "But, if he happens to read my shirt ..."

It was a little gentler than Dirty Harry's "Make my day," but in the same vein. Movie scene: A golfer steps on the first tee, draws out his weapon (a driver), looks grimly at his opponent and snaps, "Go ahead. Read my shirt ..."

An unlikely group — Doug Weaver, Jerry Pate, Nick Price and Mark Wiebe — beat the odds to become the Four Aces, all scoring holes-in-one at No. 6 within two hours, all using 7-irons.

Aussie Steve Elkington had a 70-70 start.

Caddy Bruce Edwards joined Greg Norman.

Mark Lye shot 69 in the second round.

Chris Perry's 67 was the day's second-lowest.

There was no new verb of the day. Just an old, old verb: "Precipitate." Used in a sentence: "It sure did precipitate something fierce overnight. And if it keeps precipitating like this, it might precipitate a nervous breakdown in the maintenance crew."

As the last fans left the course Friday, they noticed a familiar feeling on their heads. A damp feeling. A pitter-patter feeling. A disheartening feeling.

It was the start of more storms — more mean, vicious storms. That zany tag-team, thunder and lightning, appeared in concert most of the night in Genesee County. Result: 1.9 inches of rain at the airport; as much as three inches in parts of the county; but lucky Soak Hill took on only an additional 1.47 inches.

Five days before, an exploration crew had found the old German battleship Bismarck under 15,000 feet of water in the Atlantic Ocean. By Saturday morning, a battleship might have been hidden on the eighth fairway at Oak Hill.

"I got to the course about 7 o'clock, and I was half asleep," the aptly named Boatwright said. "That Mississippi River down No. 8 woke me up."

"That Mississippi River" was actually Allen's Creek, overflowing to become Allen's River with designs on becoming Allen's Reservoir.

A fire truck spent all morning pumping out the water — a thousand gallons a minute for three hours. Early-arriving fans walked and rode under a stream of water reminiscent of the fountains at Caesar's Palace. Only Evel and/or Robbie Knievel were missing. (Dept. of Omens: Pernice, who rep-

resents Caesar's on the tour, shot a 68 that propelled him from tie-24th to tie-seventh.)

The eighth wasn't the only hole under serious water. The fifth and seventh fairways were also inundated. Casual water was approximately everywhere else. You know the saying, "Water, water everywhere..." Stop right there. That says it all. There was fear the course might not be reparable, that Saturday's round might sleep with the fishes. Play, scheduled to start at 8:45, was rescheduled for 12:51 with groups of three rather than two, and with players going off both the first and 10th tees (an Open first). But added to the USGA announcement was an ominous note: "At 12:00 today, a final decision will be made as to whether there will be any play at all."

Somehow, they played.

Somehow, men — anonymous men — moved lakes, covered mudholes, held their breath ... and allowed other men — famous men — to play. And Sunday's newspaper headlines touted the famous men — "Major in sight for Kite;" "Familiar spot for Larry Nelson;" "Japan's Ozaki fires 68;" "Simpson right up there;" — while the real heroes went home and had a cold dinner at midnight.

At 2:35 p.m., just 35 minutes late, USGA starter Ron Read announced the leader group and said, "Play away, please." There were three, of course, instead of two, Simpson having been added to the preordained pairing of Kite and Strange.

It would be a long day for Strange in every way. He would not make a birdie. His one-shot lead would become a three-shot

A third consecutive sub-par round took Tom Kite to the top of the leaderboard.

A few of the day's heroes at work.

deficit. And he would suffer this indignity over the absurd period of five hours, 18 minutes.

Third Round

Tom Kite	69-205
Scott Simpson	69-206
Curtis Strange	73-208
Larry Nelson	68-209
Masashi Ozaki	68-209
Jay Don Blake	72-209
Tom Pernice, Jr.	68-210
Mark McCumber	72-210
Brian Claar	68-211
Jose-Maria Olazabal	70-211
Chip Beck	71-211
Ian Woosnam	73-211

It's doubtful if skilled men could play this game any slower than the field did Saturday. They blamed the wet conditions —

A fire truck took three hours, pumping a thousand gallons a minute, from the overflow of Allen's Creek. Play was scheduled to start at 8:45 a.m., but began at 12:51 p.m.

drops from casual water; plugged drives; mud globs on their balls — but basically they just turtled it.

At times, play was so s-l-o-o-o-w the Open seemed to be going backward, like Michael Jackson doing his Moon Walk.

Two groups were warned, but no penalties were meted.

The early play was uninspiring. Strange bogeyed No. 2 after hitting both a fairway bunker and a greenside bunker. Kite gave it back by missing a two-foot putt at No. 4, kissing the right lip and ramblin' on by.

An hour into the round, Strange still held a one-shot lead over Kite, Simpson and Blake. Then all three challengers bogeyed No. 5 and Strange held a two-shot lead.

An hour-and-a-half into the round, of the six men who started the day under par, not one of them had a birdie.

Open pressure, anyone?

It was reminiscent of a scene locals tell from the 1968 Open. A spectator allegedly

Photo: Michael Cohen

A 67 lifted Fred Couples in the third round.

Brian Claar was well-positioned after his 68.

Driving was the key to a 68 by Larry Nelson.

somehow wandered onto nearby Irondequoit Country Club and started watching its members play. "These are the world's best golfers?" he asked.

Finally, Blake stuck his tee shot a foot from the pin on No. 6 and the drought ended. Drought? Well, *birdie* drought.

Then, for yet another hour, nothing happened but more backward ambling. Kite nearly holed out from a bunker at No. 7. But didn't. Dan Forsman was a blip on the radar screen for a couple of minutes, battling to two-under. Then, he crashed.

However, things were happening from the rear. Satchell Paige said, "Don't look back because something might be gaining on you." It was true at Soak Hill. Peter Jacobsen and Larry Nelson were gaining (both were three-under for the day; two-under for the championship). Pernice was gaining (three-under for the day; one-under for the championship). And Jumbo Ozaki, the Japanese pro who with his caddy was

doing the greatest emoting since Hope and Crosby, was gaining (two-under for the day; one-under for the championship).

The lead became a community affair at the ninth. Kite rolled in a 40-footer for birdie, his first of the day, and Strange followed by missing a 10-foot par-saver. That left Strange, Kite and Blake at three-under.

Seconds later, Eddie Kirby one-hopped his approach into the hole at No. 12 for eagle to go two-under. Eddie Kirby? Yes. Maybe you know him as Edward Kirby. That's the way he was on the main scoreboard, but he wasn't happy with it and asked that it be changed to Eddie. "You don't put 'Thomas O. Kite' on the board, do you?" he asked.

Anyway, he's 26 and from Cumberland, Rhode Island, and in our endless search for this year's Lee Trevino, Eddie Kirby was the latest candidate.

A rain-splashed Curtis Strange putted poorly and stumbled to 73 in the third round.

It's the ball that really matters: Strange studies a putt as caddy Greg Rita keeps the ball dry.

Playing in the next-to-last group, Blake took the sole lead with a 25-footer at No. 10, and you just knew back home in that hardware store, people were banging the rakes together in some kind of Utah Symphony.

A couple of minutes later, with the last group on the 10th green, the rain came again. Pouring. Absolutely pouring. Surprised? Hey, this is the Open, isn't it? This is Rochester, isn't it? Golf fans should get medals. They are a most amazing species.

On the backside, the rain having subsided, Kite and Simpson took control. Kite birdied 10, 12 and 14, which along with his birdie on No. 9 gave him four birdies in six holes, and started to creep away. Simpson birdied 10 and 13 to stay within sight.

Tom Kite (opposite) took control on the last nine of the third round.

But Kite's birdie at 14, plus a Blake bogey at 15 (the first of three in a row) suddenly made this a three-shot ballgame — Kite six-under; Blake, Simpson and Strange three-under. (Kirby bogeyed two of the three holes after his eagle to exit the war, almost as quickly as he had entered.)

Might the little pro in the wire-rimmed glasses and the new cross-handed putting style be breaking away? The little pro who says his vision, uncorrected, is "blind."

Nope. Kite immediately three-putted 15 after yet another short but drenching rain, and Simpson rolled in a 30-foot birdie at 16. Strange made his daily bogey at 17 and then the boys went to the tent and added it all up. Kite had shot his third straight under-par round, a 69 to go with 67-69 and was five-under and leading. Simpson had also put together a 69 to go with a 67-70 and was

Scott Simpson put together a 69 and took second place after 54 holes.

Chip Beck's 71 put him in a ninth-place tie.

Peter Jacobsen also had a third-round 71.

Jumbo Ozaki's 68 gave him a share of fourth.

Jose-Maria Olazabal lived up to his billing.

four-under, one back. Strange was 71-64-73, two-under, and was off to the practice range, tampering until dark, trying to find a key for Sunday.

The leader underwent a thorough psychoanalysis by the media after the round. Kite was asked why, suddenly, he had found success in a tournament that previously had been so unkind to him. "I have a difficult time explaining my lack of success in the Open," he said, "because the Open is a tournament I should play well in. This has been a puzzling tournament for me."

Puzzling in that Kite is a straight hitter, a steady player and a par-worshipper — precisely the kind of man who should do well in Opens — yet in 17 previous tries, he had but a single Top 10 finish, had missed six cuts and had never been a factor.

Now, however, he was The Factor.

"I'll be nervous tomorrow," he said. "Every player who has a chance to win will be nervous. I anticipate it. I welcome it. I want to be nervous tomorrow. That's what we're here for."

Spectators intently watch the third-round action.

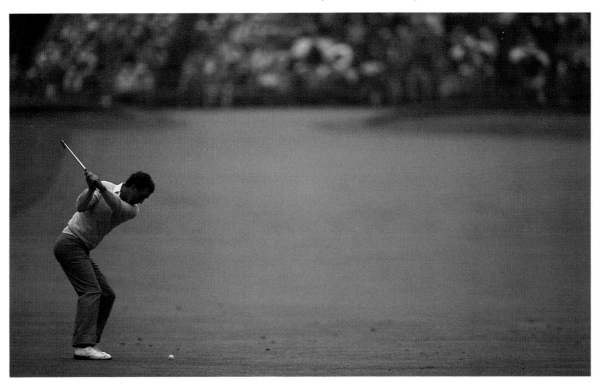

Former U.S. Open champion Hubert Green on No. 2. Green eventually tied for ninth place.

Of the Four Aces, only Mark Wiebe was close.

Paul Azinger got on track with his 70.

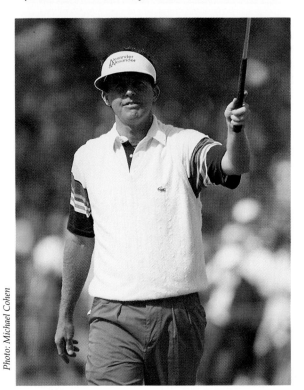

Scott Hoch was having another solid week.

After a fine start, Richard Zokol slipped to 76.

Photo: Michael Cohen

Jay Don Blake lost ground with 72.

The new verb of the day: "Three-peat."

Used in a sentence: "Curtis, now that you've repeated, do you think you can three-peat?"

Runner-up new verb of the day: "Hogan."

Used in a sentence: "Curtis really Hoganed his ball around, didn't he?"

Yes, he did.

In a marvelous display of Hoganism at its finest, Curtis Strange became the first man in 38 years to successfully defend his U.S. Open title, the first since the perfectionist himself, Ben Hogan, did it in 1951.

Strange's round was so Hoganesque, it was like a visit to the past.

Fairway, green, two-putt.

Fairway, green, two-putt.

Fairway, green, two-putt.

"It was like watching paint dry," Strange said at one point in describing his masterwork final-round even-par 70. In a way, it was. But if so, the paint was being applied by Rembrandt and that in itself made it worth watching. Birdies are the staff of life at the regular stops on the tour, but they are mere curiosities at the Open. Par is the staff of life here. And Curtis was making pars and making them like an artisan.

As he did, others fell away until he was the only one left. Kite, the third-round leader, plummeted farthest with an agonizing 78 that was like witnessing a death in the family. Marlon Brando described it best in the movie, *Apocalypse Now*: "Oh, the horror." That was Tom Kite's round in three words. "Oh, the horror."

Scott Simpson, who began the day in second, also stepped off a precipice, shooting a 75.

Curtis Strange urges on his crucial birdie putt at No. 16 to go three under par and hold a two-stroke lead.

Strange's 70 was admirable not because of its spectacle but because of its steadiness. It soared because of its earthtones. It wasn't so much that Curtis Strange seized the Open by the jugular; more that he didn't allow it to seize him.

Question: How often does that happen in the Open?

Answer: How many Opens have there been?

So he came to the 18th green again in what is becoming a familiar pose — both arms thrust high in the air, red shirt a bit wrinkled, smile at full gleam. The Open champion.

Twice over.

"I think what I did as well as anyone else," he would say later, "was have patience. It was as simple as that — patience."

As simple, and as complex.

If it were that simple, every man with a bagful of steel sticks would be dripping in it. If it were that simple, some entrepreneur would be selling it at the gate for $20, like parking spots in his front yard.

The concept of patience may be simple, but the ability to be patient is a blessing not easily obtained. When it was being passed out, however, Strange got two helpings. That's how, counting his last two holes Friday, plus Saturday's round, plus his first 15 holes Sunday, the man went 35 holes without a birdie and still maintained his composure like a neurosurgeon.

And when the birdie finally came, a 15-footer straight uphill on the 16th, it had been worth waiting for. "If one shot won the Open," he said, "that (putt) was it."

Worth waiting for and, amazingly, all he would need. Because what that single, lonesome, final-round birdie did was give Strange a two-shot cushion heading into 17 and 18, holes Chip Beck called "as tough finishing

holes as we'll ever see." Strange used one of those shots with almost a preplanned three-putt on 18 and used the other as his winning margin over Beck, Mark McCumber and Ian Woosnam.

His 70 gave him a four-day total of two-under-par 278. Each of the runners-up broke par Sunday (Woosnam 68; Beck 68; McCumber 69), but none had any round even close to Strange's Friday 64. The champion said afterward that he'll remember his Sunday round the most and that his birdie on 16 "won the Open," but it could as easily be argued his Friday frolic was his passport.

Sunday was a gas if for nothing else than the weather. Although the morning was ugly and threatening, that was just a formality. Rochester isn't allowed to have a day without a scare; it's in the city's manifest. The clouds, said the weatherman, would scud on out by early afternoon and this new, nearly unheardof atmospheric condition called sunshine would bathe the land with warmth and good will, spreading peace and prosperity among the people, and eventually, everyone would win the lottery.

OK, so maybe he just said there'd be sunshine.

Either way, there was.

So when Strange and Larry Nelson teed off at 2:01 p.m., then Kite and Simpson followed at 2:10 and there hadn't been any rain and Allen's Creek was behaving itself and women were searching through their purses for their sunglasses, well, you had to stand there, scratch your head and ask, "Uh, can this be the Open?"

Can be and is.

Kite certainly looked the part of an Oak Hill Open champion. He had donned the garb of the 1968 champion, Lee Trevino — red shirt and black pants, although he drew the line on the red socks and Band Aid on the forearm. Soon, alas, he would need a Band Aid to stop the bleeding, then a tourniquet, then a full M*A*S*H unit. But nothing would work.

Nelson hit the best shots early. He had

One of his many trouble spots, No. 8, cost Tom Kite a stroke as he shot 78 and finished tied for ninth place (opposite).

Early in the round, however, Kite was visibly confident, taking a three-stroke lead after three holes.

struggled with his iron game the day before, but now he was hitting laser-controlled missiles at the pins, five feet on No. 2, 15 feet on No. 3, eight feet on No. 4. But the man couldn't buy a putt, couldn't have bought one if Donald Trump had bankrolled him. One day the putter's your best pal but your iron shots are leaking rotten egg gas. The next day, your irons sizzle and your putter's Benedict Arnold. Ah, golf.

Kite sank a 10-footer to save par at No. 1, misread a 12-foot birdie at No. 2, then drained a 20-foot birdie at No. 3 after a gorgeous 2-iron tee shot. If this is what Open-leading nerves look like, give everyone a plateful, please. Saturday, Tom Kite said he expected to be nervous, welcomed nervousness, wanted to be nervous. So why did Tom Kite look like the calmest man in upstate New York?

As Kite was dropping the 20-footer at No. 3, his playing partner, Simpson, was making bogey after a tee shot hooked into the hinterlands. Just that quickly, at 2:47 p.m., Tom Kite had a three-shot lead with 15 holes to play. And after pars at the fourth, Tom Kite had a three-shot lead with 14 holes to play.

Then ... well, the grim reaper came and tapped Tom Kite on the shoulder ... No, that's too dramatic.

Let's try: Then ... well, the earth opened up and swallowed Tom ... No, that's still too dramatic.

Let's try: Then, Tom Kite blocked out his driver and hit one in Allen's Creek. Omnipresent Allen's Creek. Post-floodstage Allen's Creek. Open-altering Allen's Creek.

After a drop and a layup, Kite still hit a nice wedge and had a makeable 10-footer for bogey. For the next minute-and-a-half, Tom Kite was a ghost on that fifth green. He rolled his first putt 18 inches past. He punched the next two feet past. He made that one. He had three-putted from 10 feet. He had triple-bogeyed. He had opened the Open to all comers.

Jumbo Ozaki (opposite) delighted the crowd with his golf and his mannerisms. He finished with a share of sixth place.

ABC's commentary team included Jack Whitaker, Jim McKay, Dave Marr, Frank Hannigan and Peter Alliss in the booth plus Bob Rosburg, Judy Rankin, Jerry Pate and Ed Sneed on the course.

He had invited everyone back to the party. They said hello, and Tom said good-bye.

The next couple of hours it became The Casey Stengel Open. "Can't anybody here play this game?"

Kite bogeyed eight and 10. Simpson doubled eight and bogeyed nine. McCumber

---

Fourth Round

Curtis Strange	70-278
Ian Woosnam	68-279
Mark McCumber	69-279
Chip Beck	68-279
Brian Claar	69-280
Masashi Ozaki	72-281
Scott Simpson	75-281
Peter Jacobsen	70-282
Jose-Maria Olazabal	72-283
Hubert Green	68-283
Tom Kite	78-283
Paul Azinger	70-283

---

bogeyed nine and 13. Woosnam doubled nine. Nelson bogeyed 10 and doubled 11.

Only Strange, like the band on the Titanic, played on. *Nearer My Championship to Thee.*

Fairway, green, two-putt.

Fairway, green, two-putt.

Fairway, green, two-putt.

"Like watching paint dry."

The present and future champion took the lead for good as he was playing toward his 13th consecutive par. Up ahead, co-leader Jumbo Ozaki pushed his drive behind a tree on 14, sailed his approach over the green and made bogey.

At that point, The Par Machine stood alone at two-under; Kite, Simpson, Beck and Ozaki were at one-under and Woosie, McCumber and Tom Pernice were even. That's eight men within two shots of the lead. Seven of them were being teased.

Oak Hill, burned by 21 sub-par rounds Thursday and by Strange's 64 Friday, was now showing her nasty side. Bogeys rained down like arrows at Thermopylae.

Kite concluded his implosion with doubles

Ian Woosnam (opposite) holed an eight-foot putt at 18 for 68 and a share of second place at 279.

A double bogey and five bogeys hurt Scott Simpson, who fell to 75 and a sixth-place tie.

at 13 and 15, trying to gouge a 4-wood out of a nearly buried lie in the rough at 13 and barely moving the ball in one final bow to reason. Simpson bogeyed 14 and 15. Ozaki bogeyed 14 and 16. Pernice bogeyed 15.

As Strange lined up his 15-foot birdie try at the 16th, he was still two-under, where he had been for the past 22 hours. Beck and Woosnam had finished at one-under and McCumber was one-under with one hole to play.

When Strange's putt dropped, so did the hopes of that trio. McCumber knew he had to birdie 18 and hope for a Strange bogey at 17 and/or 18. McCumber got it to 20 feet at 18, but faced what he called "the severest pin in the 72 holes of the Open." He two-putted for par.

And, when Strange parred 17 for the first time all week, he was two up with one to play, making his three-putt at 18 meaningless.

The runners-up were effusive with their praise, none more so than Beck. "Curtis obviously has a lot of inner strength, a lot of tenacity and a lot of courage to pull that off,"

he said.

And no one felt worse than Kite. "My play stunk," he said. "There's not much you can say about it. This is kind of what the U.S. Open is about. But I'll survive this, I promise you."

Finally, the champion spoke.

"Move over, Ben," he said first.

"I do not know Mr. Hogan," Strange said. "I have never met him. Obviously, as great a player as he was, it's a good feeling to do this — not so much what Ben Hogan did, but what no one else since did. Not the great Arnold Palmer, not the great Jack Nicklaus, not the great Tom Watson. I put a lot of weight in that it hasn't been done in so long."

"Do you feel like the best player in the world?" a man asked.

"Naw," Curtis Strange said, "I just feel like the guy who won the U.S. Open."

That's plenty.

Mark McCumber (opposite) had this 20-foot birdie attempt at No. 18. His 69 and 279 total was one stroke off the winning pace.

Chip Beck shot 68 and was an Open runner-up for the second time. He also was tied for second behind Raymond Floyd in the 1986 Open at Shinnecock Hills.

Curtis Strange kept the lead with a par at the 15th hole. It was his 35th consecutive without a birdie.

89th U.S. OPEN CHAMPIONSHIP

START	LEADERS	PAR	1	2	3	4	5	6	7	8	9	10	11	12	13	14	15	16	17	18	MESSAGES
	HOLE		4	4	3	5	4	3	4	4	4	4	3	4	5	4	3	4	4	4	
2	STRANGE		2	2	2	2	2	2	2	2	2	2	2	2	2	2	3	3	2		HAPPY
4	SIMPSON S		4	4	3	3	3	3	3	1	0	0	0	1	1	0	1	0	0		FATHER'S
1	ZAKI			1	2	2	0	0	0	1	1	2	2	2	1	1	0	0	1		DAY
1	K C		1	0	1	1	2	2	2	1	1	1	0	1	1	1	1	1	1		
1	SNAM		0	1	1	1	1	1	1	1	1	0	0	0	0	1	0	0	1		
0	UMBER		0	0	0	1	1	1	1	2	1	1	1	1	0	0	0	1	1		
	R		2	2	3	2	2	2	3	3	2	2	1	1	1	1	2	1	0		
0	NICE		0	0	0	1	1	1	0	0	0	0	0	0	0	0	1	1	4		

Once Strange's final number was on the scoreboard, it was only a matter of time.

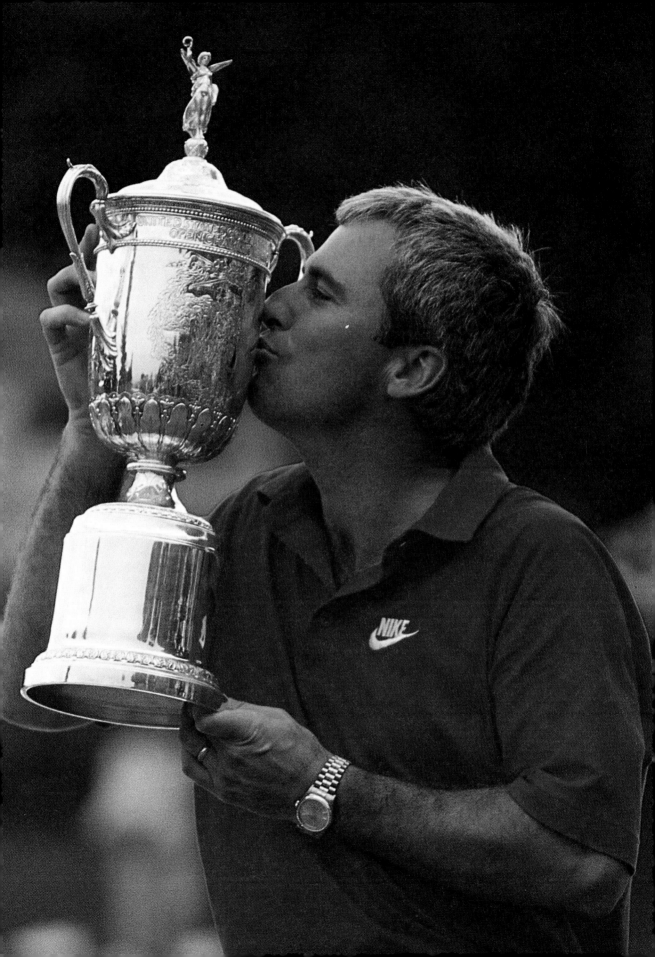

**89th
U. S. Open**

The Champion

It was Monday, April 15, the Monday after the 1985 Masters.

Curtis Strange had blown the Masters the day before. There are a lot of nicer ways to put it — like, "He let it slip away" — but none does the job like "He'd blown it." Leading by four going to the back nine, Strange plunked shots in the creek at 13 and in the lake at 15, shot a 39 and lost by two to Bernhard Langer.

Now he was at one of those company outings that dot the top players' Monday schedules, this one in Bristol, Tennessee. Strange played in the afternoon, had dinner with the company's VIPs and clients, made a short speech and asked, "Anyone have any questions?"

The only noises in the room were some nervous coughs.

"Then I asked, 'Did anybody watch TV yesterday?' and a hundred hands went up," Curtis Strange said, laughing. "I answered questions for the next hour."

This had been another historical minute in the coming of age of Curtis Strange.

If Strange always has had that side of him — and those who know him well say he has — he didn't put it on display very often. He grew up with an angry veneer, and he had a tendency to show it too often in the early years of his career.

An incident at Bay Hill in 1982 is the most famous but not the only one. Strange cussed out a lady scorekeeper in words usually saved for backrooms of bars. The subsequent uproar was a turning point in his career and, in fact, his life. He knew who he was, but now he was finally realizing that others didn't. He knew he wasn't an ogre, but he saw that was his image. And for once, he cared.

Bill Millsaps, sports editor of the *Richmond Times-Dispatch*, tells of an incident the year before that at the Masters. Strange had shot 69-79 and was flinging stuff around the lockerroom. Millsaps was trying to get a couple of quotes, but Strange wasn't cooperating. Finally, Millsaps walked out. "He sat down in the Atlanta airport and wrote me a letter of apology for the way he acted," Millsaps said. "I've been in the business 26 years and only two people have ever done that."

So he could be rude, but there was always another side to Curtis Strange, even before he climbed to the top of the tour money list, a place he has inhabited three of the past four years.

When he won in 1988 at Brookline, he broke down at the memory of his father, who died of cancer when Curtis was 14. This time he said the victory was for himself, his wife, Sarah, and their two sons.

"The difference in golf tournaments," Strange said, "was last year was such an emotional victory and that was for my Dad, and everybody else that had helped me along, and my friends. But this one is for me and Sarah and Thomas and David. They are as much a part of me winning this golf tournament as anybody, because you sacrifice a lot to play this tour. I sacrifice and they do, too. So it is a team effort. I couldn't do it without them."

Then he pinpointed what it took to win. "To go as long as I did without a birdie, I like to think it's intestinal fortitude ... or guts," he said. "Invariably, year after year, that's what it takes to win the Open. It's a marathon in a lot of ways. You have to persevere, and that's what I did."

The point was not even arguable. A roomful of media just sat nodding their heads. Yup.

But where did he get this fortitude, this will, this attitude of "You will not beat me."

"I was born with it," Strange said matter-of-factly, "and I nurtured it along. You can teach it, but only so much."

Chandler Harper, a former PGA champion and one of the men who filled in as father figure after Tom Strange died, saw it long ago, too. "I think his biggest asset is his fierce desire to win," Harper said in *Golf Magazine* in 1978. "That will take him a long way."

"I just feel if it comes down to, 'Who wants it more?' I want it a bunch," Strange said. "I think a lot of it comes down to having a mean streak."

No one would ever argue Curtis doesn't have one of them. A mean streak, a contrary streak, an obstinate streak. Some call it the "killer instinct."

Curtis Strange calls his own plays. He doesn't have a coach sending them in from the sideline. He wears no masks. What you see, you get.

Strange's college coach at Wake Forest was Jesse Haddock. He is the man who saw the future. "I've had a lot of young fellows with great potential," Haddock said way back when. "I think this is one who can become a superstar."

The point is not even arguable. Just sit there and nod your head. Yup.

The delight of Curtis and Sarah Strange was obvious, but this was a less emotional victory.

Hole	1	2	3	4	5	6	7	8	9	10	11	12	13	14	15	16	17	18	Total
Par	4	4	3	5	4	3	4	4	4	4	3	4	5	4	3	4	4	4	70	

Curtis Strange

	1	2	3	4	5	6	7	8	9	10	11	12	13	14	15	16	17	18	Total	
Round 1	4	4	3	5	5	2	4	4	4	5	3	3	5	4	3	4	6	3	71	
Round 2	3	3	3	3	4	3	4	4	4	3	3	4	5	3	3	3	5	4	64	
Round 3	4	5	3	5	4	3	4	4	5	4	3	4	5	4	3	4	5	4	73	
Round 4	4	4	3	5	4	3	4	4	4	4	3	4	5	4	3	3	4	5	70	278

Chip Beck

	1	2	3	4	5	6	7	8	9	10	11	12	13	14	15	16	17	18	Total	
Round 1	4	4	3	4	4	3	4	5	4	4	3	3	5	5	3	4	5	4	71	
Round 2	5	3	3	4	4	2	4	4	4	4	3	4	5	4	3	4	4	5	69	
Round 3	4	3	3	5	4	3	4	6	3	4	3	4	5	4	4	3	5	4	71	
Round 4	4	3	4	5	5	3	4	3	4	4	2	3	5	4	3	4	4	4	68	279

Mark McCumber

	1	2	3	4	5	6	7	8	9	10	11	12	13	14	15	16	17	18	Total	
Round 1	4	4	3	5	3	2	4	4	4	4	3	4	5	4	2	4	5	6	70	
Round 2	4	3	2	5	4	4	4	4	4	5	3	4	5	4	2	3	4	4	68	
Round 3	4	4	3	5	5	3	4	4	5	3	3	4	5	4	3	5	4	4	72	
Round 4	4	4	3	4	4	3	4	3	5	4	3	4	6	4	3	3	4	4	69	279

Ian Woosnam

	1	2	3	4	5	6	7	8	9	10	11	12	13	14	15	16	17	18	Total	
Round 1	3	4	4	4	5	3	4	4	4	5	2	4	5	4	3	4	4	4	70	
Round 2	3	4	3	5	4	3	4	4	3	4	2	5	5	3	2	5	5	4	68	
Round 3	4	4	3	5	4	4	4	4	4	5	3	4	5	4	3	5	4	4	73	
Round 4	3	3	3	5	4	3	4	4	6	3	3	4	5	5	2	4	4	3	68	279

Hole	Par	Eagles	Birdies	Pars	Bogeys	Higher	Rank	Average
1	4	1	40	275	119	19	7	4.26
2	4	0	65	293	88	8	13	4.09
3	3	0	33	278	130	13	6	3.27
4	5	1	113	241	90	9	18	4.98
5	4	0	32	252	135	34	2	4.39
6	3	4	73	301	67	8	17	3.00
7	4	0	36	275	118	24	4	4.29
8	4	0	47	265	126	15	8	4.24
9	4	0	44	293	106	10	10	4.19
OUT	35	6	483	2473	979	140		36.71
10	4	0	49	248	136	20	4	4.29
11	3	0	65	314	67	7	16	3.04
12	4	1	62	292	88	10	12	4.10
13	5	0	62	319	61	11	15	5.05
14	4	0	60	304	83	6	14	4.08
15	3	0	78	258	97	20	11	3.13
16	4	0	46	284	108	15	9	4.21
17	4	1	23	211	189	29	1	4.50
18	4	0	39	258	140	16	3	4.30
IN	35	2	484	2488	969	134		36.70
TOTAL	70	8	967	4961	1948	274		73.41

Date	Winner, Runner-Up	Score	Site	Entry
1895 (Oct.)	**Horace Rawlins**	173	**Newport G.C.,**	11
	Willie Dunn	175	Newport R.I.	
1896 (July)	**James Foulis**	†152	**Shinnecock Hills G.C.,**	35
	Horace Rawlins	155	Southampton, N.Y.	
1897 (Sept.)	**Joe Lloyd**	162	**Chicago, G.C.,**	35
	Willie Anderson	163	Wheaton, Ill.	
1898 (June)	**Fred Herd**	328	**Myopia Hunt Club,**	49
	Alex Smith	335	S. Hamilton, Mass.	
1899 (Sept.)	**Willie Smith**	315	**Baltimore C.C.,**	81
	George Low/Val Fitzjohn/W.H. Way	326	(Roland Park Course) Baltimore, Md.	
1900 (Oct.)	**Harry Vardon**	313	**Chicago G.C.,**	60
	J.H. Taylor	315	Wheaton, Ill.	
1901 (June)	**Willie Anderson**	331-85	**Myopia Hunt Club,**	60
	Alex Smith	331-86	S. Hamilton, Mass.	
1902 (Oct.)	**Lawrence Auchterlonie**	307	**Garden City, G.C.,**	90
	Stewart Gardner/*Walter J. Travis	313	Garden City, N.Y.	
1903 (June)	**Willie Anderson**	307-82	**Baltusrol G.C.,**	89
	David Brown	307-84	(original course) Springfield, N.J.	
1904 (July)	**Willie Anderson**	303	**Glen View Club,**	71
	Gilbert Nicholls	308	Golf, Ill.	
1905 (Sept.)	**Willie Anderson**	314	**Myopia Hunt Club,**	83
	Alex Smith	316	S. Hamilton, Mass.	
1906 (June)	**Alex Smith**	295	**Onwentsia Club,**	68
	William Smith	302	Lake Forest, Ill.	
1907 (June)	**Alex Ross**	302	**Philadelphia Cricket C.,**	82
	Gilbert Nicholls	304	(St. Martins Course) Philadelphia, Pa.	
1908 (Aug.)	**Fred McLeod**	322-77	**Myopia Hunt Club,**	88
	Willie Smith	322-83	S. Hamilton, Mass.	
1909 (June)	**George Sargent**	290	**Englewood G.C.,**	84
	Tom McNamara	294	Englewood, N.Y.	
1910 (June)	**Alex Smith**	298-71	**Philadelphia Cricket C.,**	75
	John J. McDermott	298-75	(St. Martins Course) Philadelphia, Pa.	
	Macdonald Smith	298-77		
1911 (June)	**John J. McDermott**	307-80	**Chicago G.C.,**	79
	Michael J. Brady	307-82	Wheaton, Ill.	
	George O. Simpson	307-85		
1912 (Aug.)	**John J. McDermott**	294	**C.C. of Buffalo**	131
	Tom McNamara	296	Buffalo, N.Y.	
1913 (Sept.)	***Francis Ouimet**	304-72	**The Country Club**	165
	Harry Vardon	304-77	Brookline, Mass.	
	Edward Ray	304-78		
1914 (Aug.)	**Walter Hagen**	290	**Midlothian C.C.,**	129
	*Charles Evans, Jr.	291	Blue Island, Ill.	
1915 (June)	***Jerone D. Travers**	297	**Baltusrol G.C.,**	141
	Tom McNamara	298	(original course,) Springfield, N.J.	
1916 (June)	***Charles Evans, Jr.**	286	**Minikahda Club,**	94
	Jock Hutchinson	288	Minneapolis, Minn.	
1917-18 — No Championships: World War I				
1919 (June)	**Walter Hagen**	301-77	**Brae Burn C.C.,**	142
	Michael J. Brady	301-78	West Newton, Mass.	
1920 (Aug.)	**Edward Ray**	295	**Inverness Club,**	265
	Harry Vardon/Jack Burke, Sr./	296	Toledo, Ohio	
	Leo Diegel/Jock Hutchison			
1921 (July)	**James M. Barnes**	289	**Columbia C.C.,**	262
	Walter Hagen/Fred McLeod	298	Chevy Chase, Md.	
1922 (July)	**Gene Sarazen**	288	**Skokie C.C.,**	323
	*Robert T. Jones, Jr./John L. Black	289	Glencoe, Ill.	
1923 (July)	***Robert T. Jones, Jr.**	296-76	**Inwood C.C.,**	360
	Bobby Cruickshank	296-78	Inwood, N.Y.	

Date	Winner, Runner-Up	Score	Site	Entry
1924 (June)	**Cyril Walker** *Robert T. Jones, Jr.	297 300	**Oakland Hills C.C.,** (South Course) Birmingham, Mich.	319
1925 (June)	**William Macfarlane** *Robert T. Jones, Jr.	291-75-72 291-75-73	**Worcester C.C.,** Worcester, Mass.	445
1926 (June)	***Robert T. Jones, Jr.** Joe Turnesa	293 294	**Scioto C.C.,** Columbus, Ohio	694
1927 (June)	**Tommy Armour** Harry Cooper	301-76 301-79	**Oakmont C.C.,** Oakmont, Pa.	898
1928 (June)	**Johnny Farrell** *Robert T. Jones, Jr.	294-143 294-144	**Olympia Fields C.C.,** (No. 4 Course) Mateson, Ill.	1,064
1929 (June)	***Robert T. Jones, Jr.** Al Espinosa	294-141 294-164	**Winged Foot G.C.,** (West Course) Mamaroneck, N.Y.	1,000
1930 (July)	***Robert T. Jones, Jr.** Macdonald Smith	287 289	**Interlachen C.C.,** Minneapolis, Minn.	1,177
1931 (July)	**Billy Burke** George Von Elm	292-149-148 292-149-149	**Inverness Club,** Toledo, Ohio	1,141
1932 (June)	**Gene Sarazen** Bobby Cruickshank/T. Philip Perkins	286 289	**Fresh Meadow C.C.,** Flushing, N.Y.	1,011
1933 (June)	***John Goodman** Ralph Guldahl	287 288	**North Shore, C.C.,** Glenview, Ill.	915
1934 (June)	**Olin Dutra** Gene Sarazen	293 294	**Merion Cricket C.,** (East Course) Ardmore, Pa.	1,063
1935 (June)	**Sam Parks, Jr.** Jimmy Thomson	299 301	**Oakmont C.C.,** Oakmont, Pa.	1,125
1936 (June)	**Tony Manero** Harry Cooper	282 284	**Baltusrol G.C.,** (Upper Course) Springfield, N.Y.	1,277
1937 (June)	**Ralph Guldahl** Sam Snead	281 283	**Oakland Hills C.C.,** (South Course) Birmingham, Mich.	1,402
1938 (June)	**Ralph Guldahl** Dick Metz	284 290	**Cherry Hills C.C.,** Englewood, Colo.	1,223
1939 (June)	**Byron Nelson** Craig Wood Denny Shute	284-68-70 284-68-73 284-76	**Philadelphia C.C.,** (Spring Mill Course) West Conshohocken, Pa.	1,193
1940 (June)	**Lawson Little** Gene Sarazen	287-70 287-73	**Canterbury, G.C.,** Cleveland, Ohio	1,161
1941 (June)	**Craig Wood** Denny Shute	284 287	**Colonial Club,** Fort Worth, Tex.	1,048
1942-45 — No Championships: World War II				
1946 (June)	**Lloyd Mangrum** Byron Nelson/Victor Ghezzi	284-72-72 284-72-73	**Canterbury, G.C.,** Cleveland, Ohio	1,175
1947 (June)	**Lew Worsham** Sam Snead	282-69 282-70	**St. Louis G.C.,** Clayton, Mo.	1,356
1948 (June)	**Ben Hogan** Jimmy Demaret	276 278	**Riviera C.C.,** Los Angeles, Calif.	1,411
1949 (June)	**Cary Middlecoff** Sam Snead/Clayton Heafner	286 287	**Medinah C.C.,** (No. 3 Course) Medinah, Ill.	1,348
1950 (June)	**Ben Hogan** Lloyd Mangrum George Fazio	287-69 287-73 287-75	**Merion G.C.,** (East Course) Ardmore, Pa.	1,379
1951 (June)	**Ben Hogan** Clayton Heafner	287 289	**Oakland Hills C.C.,** (South Course) Birmingham, Mich.	1,511
1952 (June)	**Julius Boros** Ed (Porky) Oliver	281 285	**Northwood Club,** Dallas, Tex.	1,688
1953 (June)	**Ben Hogan** Sam Snead	283 289	**Oakmont C.C.,** Oakmont, Pa.	1,669
1954 (June)	**Ed Furgol** Gene Littler	284 285	**Baltusrol G.C.,** (Lower Course) Springfield, N. J.	1,928
1955 (June)	**Jack Fleck** Ben Hogan	287-69 287-72	**Olympic Club,** (Lake Course) San Francisco, Calif.	1,522
1956 (June)	**Cary Middlecoff** Julius Boros/Ben Hogan	281 282	**Oak Hill C.C.,** (East Course) Rochester, N.Y.	1,921
1957 (June)	**Dick Mayer** Cary Middlecoff	282-72 282-79	**Inverness Club,** Toledo, Ohio	1,907
1958 (June)	**Tommy Bolt** Gary Player	283 287	**Southern Hills C.C.,** Tulsa, Okla.	2,132
1959 (June)	**Bill Casper, Jr.** Bob Rosburg	282 283	**Winged Foot G.C.,** (West Course) Mamaroneck, N.Y.	2,385

Date	Winners, Runner-Up	Score	Site	Entry
1960 (June)	**Arnold Palmer** *Jack Nicklaus	280 282	**Cherry Hills C.C.,** Englewood, Colo.	2,453
1961 (June)	**Gene Littler** Doug Sanders/Bob Goalby	281 282	**Oakland Hills C.C.,** (South Course) Birmingham, Mich.	2,449
1962 (June)	**Jack Nicklaus** Arnold Palmer	283-71 283-74	**Oakmont, C.C.,** Oakmont, Pa.	2,475
1963 (June)	**Julius Boros** Jacky Cupit Arnold Palmer	293-70 293-73 293-76	**The Country Club** Brookline, Mass.	2,392
1964 (June)	**Ken Venturi** Tommy Jacobs	278 282	**Congressional C.C.,** Washington, D.C.	2,341
1965 (June)	**Gary Player** Kel Nagel	282-71 282-74	**Bellerive C.C.,** St. Louis, Mo.	2,271
1966 (June)	**Bill Casper, Jr.** Arnold Palmer	278-69 278-73	**Olympic Club,** (Lake Course) San Francisco, Calif.	2,475
1967 (June)	**Jack Nicklaus** Arnold Palmer	275 279	**Baltusrol G.C.,** (Lower Course) Springfield, N.J.	2,651
1968 (June)	**Lee Trevino** Jack Nicklaus	275 279	**Oak Hill C.C.,** (East Course) Rochester, N.Y.	3,007
1969 (June)	**Orville Moody** Deane Beman/Al Geiberger/Bob Rosburg	281 282	**Champions G.C.,** (Cypress Creek Course) Houston, Tex.	3,397
1970 (June)	**Tony Jacklin** Dave Hill	281 288	**Hazeltine National G.C.,** Chaska, Minn.	3,605
1971 (June)	**Lee Trevino** Jack Nicklaus	280-68 280-71	**Merion G.C.,** (East Course) Ardmore, Pa.	4,279
1972 (June)	**Jack Nicklaus** Bruce Crampton	290 293	**Pebble Beach G.L.,** Pebble Beach, Calif.	4,196
1973 (June)	**John Miller** John Schlee	279 280	**Oakmont C.C.,** Oakmont, Pa.	3,580
1974 (June)	**Hale Irwin** Forrest Fezler	287 289	**Winged Foot G.C.,** (West Course) Mamaroneck, N.Y.	3,914
1975 (June)	**Lou Graham** John Mahaffey	287-71 287-73	**Medinah C.C.,** (No. 3 Course) Medinah, Ill.	4,214
1976 (June)	**Jerry Pate** Tom Weiskopf/Al Geiberger	277 279	**Atlanta Athletic C.,** Duluth, Ga.	4,436
1977 (June)	**Hubert Green** Lou Graham	278 279	**Southern Hills C.C.,** Tulsa, Okla.	4,608
1978 (June)	**Andy North** J.C. Snead/Dave Stockton	285 286	**Cherry Hills C.C.,** Englewood, Colo.	4,897
1979 (June)	**Hale Irwin** Gary Player/Jerry Pate	284 286	**Inverness Club,** Toledo, Ohio	4,853
1980 (June)	**Jack Nicklaus** Isao Aoki	†272 274	**Baltusrol G.C.,** (Lower Course) Springfield, N. J.	4,812
1981 (June)	**David Graham** Bill Rogers/George Burns	273 276	**Merion G.C.,** (East Course) Ardmore, Pa.	4,946
1982 (June)	**Tom Watson** Jack Nicklaus	282 284	**Pebble Beach G.L.,** Pebble Beach, Calif.	5,255
1983 (June)	**Larry Nelson** Tom Watson	280 281	**Oakmont C.C.,** Oakmont, Pa.	5,039
1984 (June)	**Fuzzy Zoeller** Greg Norman	276-67 276-75	**Winged Foot G.C.,** (West Course) Mamaroneck, N.Y.	5,195
1985 (June)	**Andy North** Chen Tze-Chung/Denis Watson/Dave Barr	279 280	**Oakland Hills C.C.,** (South Course) Birmingham, Mich.	5,274
1986 (June)	**Raymond Floyd** Lanny Wadkins/Chip Beck	279 281	**Shinnecock Hills G.C.,** Southampton, N.Y.	5,410
1987 (June)	**Scott Simpson** Tom Watson	277 278	**Olympic Club,** (Lake Course) San Francisco, Calif.	5,696
1988 (June)	**Curtis Strange** Nick Faldo	278-71 278-75	**The Country Club,** Brookline, Mass.	5,775
1989 (June)	**Curtis Strange** Chip Beck/Mark McCumber/Ian Woosnam	278 279	**Oak Hill C.C.,** (East Course) Rochester, N.Y.	§5,786

†Record Score   *Denotes Amateur   § Record Entry

1917 — An Open Patriotic Tournament was conducted by the USGA for the benefit of the American Red Cross at the Whitemarsh Valley Country Club, Philadelphia, Pa., June 20-22. Winner: Jock Hutchinson, 292; runner-up: Tom McNamara, 299.

1942 — A Hale America Tournament was conducted by the USGA in cooperation with the Chicago District Golf Association and the Professional Golfers' Association of America for the benefit of the Navy Relief Society and the United Service Organization at Ridgemoor Country Club, Chicago, Ill., June 18-21. Winner: Ben Hogan, 271; runners-up: Jimmy Demaret and Mike Turnesa, 274.

89th U.S. Open
Championship Records

Amateurs: Champions — Francis Ouimet (1913); Jerome D. Travers (1915); Charles Evans, Jr. (1916); Robert T. Jones, Jr. (1923-26-29-30); John Goodman (1933).

Amateurs: Lowest 18-Hole Score — 65 by James B. McHale in third round in 1947, and James Simons in third round in 1971.

Amateurs: Lowest 72-Hole Scores — 282 by Jack Nicklaus in 1960; 283, James Simons in 1971.

Best Comebacks — 18 Holes: Jack Fleck in 1955 was nine strokes off the pace and came back to win.

36 Holes — Lou Graham in 1975 was 11 strokes behind.

54 Holes — Arnold Palmer in 1960 was seven strokes behind. John Miller in 1973 was six strokes behind.

63 Holes — Billy Casper was seven strokes behind Arnold Palmer with nine holes to play in 1966. Casper shot 32 on the incoming nine, Palmer shot 39.

Best Start by Champion — 63 by Jack Nicklaus in 1980.

Best Finish by Champion — 63 by John Miller in 1973. Second low is 65 by Arnold Palmer in 1960, Jack Nicklaus in 1967 and Fuzzy Zoeller in a playoff in 1984.

Champions Who Led All the Way — Only four have led after every round. Walter Hagen in 1914, Jim Barnes in 1921, Ben Hogan in 1953 and Tony Jacklin in 1970. Seven other champions have led or were in a tie all the way — Willie Anderson in 1903, Alex Smith in 1906, Charles Evans, Jr., in 1916, Tommy Bolt in 1958, Jack Nicklaus in 1972 and 1980, and Hubert Green in 1977.

Clubs Most Often Host — Baltusrol Golf Club, Springfield, N.J., and Oakmont Country Club, Oakmont, Pa., six times. Opens were played at Baltusrol in 1903, 1915, 1936, 1954, 1967 and 1980, and at Oakmont in 1927, 1935, 1953, 1962, 1973 and 1983. Oakland Hills Country Club, Birmingham, Mich., has been host to the Open five times, in 1924, 1937, 1951, 1961 and 1985.

Consecutive Winners — Six players: Willie Anderson (1903-04-05); John J. McDermott (1911-12); Robert T. Jones, Jr. (1929-30); Ralph Guldahl (1937-38); Ben Hogan (1950-51) and Curtis Strange (1988-89).

Entry Record — 5,786 in 1989.

Finishes in First Ten — 18 by Jack Nicklaus. Walter Hagen finished in the first ten 16 times; Ben Hogan 15 times.

First Score in 60s — David Hunter, of Essex Country Club, West Orange, N.J., returned a card of 68 in the first round of the 1909 Championship. He finished with 313 and in a tie for 30th.

Foreign Winners — David Graham, of Australia, became the 20th foreign-born winner in 1981. However, 16 of the 20 had already emigrated to the United States before they won. The four overseas champions were Harry Vardon of England in 1900, Ted Ray of England in 1920, Gary Player of South Africa in 1965, and Tony Jacklin of England in 1970.

Foreign Players' Best 72-Hole Scores — 273 — David Graham in 1981; 274 — Isao Aoki in 1980; 276 — Greg Norman in 1984; 279 — Ian Woosnam in 1989; 280 — Chen Tze-Chung, Denis Watson and Dave Barr in 1985; 281 — Tony Jacklin in 1970, Masashi Ozaki in 1989; 282 — Gary Player and Kel Nagle in 1965, Bobby Locke in 1948, Seve Ballesteros in 1987.

Highest Scores to Lead Field, 18 Holes — All-time high is 89 by Willie Dunn, James Foulis, and Willie Campbell in 1895. Since World War II, high is 71 in 1951, 1958, 1970 and 1972.

Highest Scores to Lead Field, 36 Holes — All-time high is 173 by Horace Rawlins in 1895. (This was a 36-hole Open.) Since World War II, high is 144 in 1951, 1955 and 1972.

Highest Scores to Lead Field, 54 Holes — All-time high is 249 by Stewart Gardner in 1901. Since World War II, high is 218 in 1951 and 1963.

Highest Scores to Lead Field, 72 Holes — All-time high is 331 by Willie Anderson and Alex Smith in 1901; Anderson won the playoff. More recent high is 299 by Sam Parks, Jr., in 1935. The post-World War II high is 293 by Julius Boros, Jacky Cupit and Arnold Palmer in 1963; Boros won the playoff.

Highest 72-Hole Score — Professional John Harrison, 393, in 1900.

Highest 36-Hole Cut — 155 in 1955 (low 50 and ties).

Lowest 9-Hole Score — 30 by Scott Simpson on the first nine of the second round in 1988; by Peter Jacobsen on the first nine of the fourth round in 1988; by Paul Azinger on the first nine of the fourth round in 1988; by Danny Edwards on the second nine of the second round in 1986; by Lennie Clements on the first nine of the third round in 1986; by Chip Beck on the second nine of the fourth round in 1986; by George Burns on the first nine of the second round in 1982; by Raymond Floyd on the first nine of the first round in 1980; by Tom Shaw in the first round and Bob Charles in the last round in 1971, both on the first nine; by Steve Spray on the second nine of the fourth round in 1968; by Ken Venturi on the first nine of the third round in 1964; by Arnold Palmer on the first nine of the final round in 1960; and by amateur James B. McHale, Jr., on the first nine of the third round in 1947.

Lowest Round — 63 by Jack Nicklaus and Tom Weiskopf (first round) over the Lower Course of the Baltusrol Golf Club, Springfield, N.J., in 1980; by John Miller (final round) at Oakmont Country Club, Oakmont, Pa., in 1973.

Lowest First Round — 63 by Jack Nicklaus and Tom Weiskopf, at the Baltusrol Golf Club, Springfield, N.J., in 1980.

Lowest Second Round — 64 by Tommy Jacobs, Congressional Country Club, Bethesda, Md., in 1964; by Rives McBee, Olympic Club, San Francisco, in 1966; by Curtis Strange, Oak Hill Country Club, Rochester, N.Y., in 1989.

Lowest Third Round — 64 by Ben Crenshaw, Merion Golf Club, Ardmore, Pa., in 1981; by Keith Clearwater, Olympic Club, San Francisco, in 1987.

Lowest Fourth Round — 63 by John Miller, Oakmont (Pa.) Country Club, in 1973.

Lowest First 36 Holes — 134 by Jack Nicklaus in 1980 and Chen Tze Chung in 1985.

Lowest Last 36 Holes — 132 by Larry Nelson in 1983.

Lowest First 54 Holes — 203 by George Burns in 1981 and Chen Tze Chung in 1985. 204 by Jack Nicklaus and Isao Aoki in 1980.

Lowest Last 54 Holes — 204 by Jack Nicklaus in 1967.

Lowest 36-Hole Cut — 145 in 1989 (low 60 and ties); 146 in 1980 and 1985 (low 60 and ties); 147 in 1960 (low 50 and ties).

Lowest 72-Hole Scores — 272 — Jack Nicklaus (63-71-70-68) in 1980; 273 — David Graham (68-68-70-67) in 1981; 274 — Isao Aoki (68-68-68-70) in 1980;

275 — Jack Nicklaus (71-67-72-65) in 1967; and Lee Trevino (69-68-69-69) in 1968.

Most Consecutive Birdies — Six by George Burns, who birdied the second through the seventh holes in the second round at Pebble Beach (Calif.) Golf Links in 1982.

Most Consecutive Opens — Jack Nicklaus has played in 33 consecutive Opens from 1957 through 1989. Gene Sarazen played in 31 successive Opens from 1920 through 1954 (no Championship 1942-45). Arnold Palmer played in 31 successive Opens from 1953 through 1983.

Most Victories — Four men have won four times: Willie Anderson (1901-03-04-05), Robert T. Jones, Jr. (1923-26-29-30), Ben Hogan (1948-50-51-53), Jack Nicklaus (1962-67-72-80).

Most Times Runner-up — Sam Snead, Robert T. Jones, Jr., Arnold Palmer and Jack Nicklaus, four times each.

Most Decisive Victories — 11 strokes — Willie Smith in 1899. Nine strokes — Jim Barnes in 1921.

Most Sub-Par Rounds in Career — 31 by Jack Nicklaus; 18 by Ben Hogan; 17 by Sam Snead and Lee Trevino.

Most Rounds Under 70 in Career — 26 by Jack Nicklaus; 15 by Arnold Palmer; Ben Hogan had 14.

Most Strokes on One Hole — Ray Ainsley took 19 strokes on the par-four sixteenth in the second round at the Cherry Hills Club, Englewood, Colo., in 1938.

Oldest Champion — Raymond Floyd was 43 years, eight months and 11 days old, when he won in 1986; Ted Ray was 43 years, four months and 16 days old, when he won in 1920; Julius Boros, the third oldest, was 26 days younger than Ted Ray on the day he won the Championship in 1963.

Pace-Setters with Largest Leads, 18 Holes — Five strokes - Tommy Armour in 1933.

Pace-Setters with Largest Leads, 36 Holes — Five strokes - Willie Anderson in 1903.

Pace-Setters with Largest Leads, 54 Holes — Seven strokes - Jim Barnes in 1921.

Poorest Start for Champion — The all-time high is 91 by Horace Rawlins in 1895. The post-World War II high is 76 by Ben Hogan in 1951 and Jack Fleck in 1955.

Poorest Finish for Champion — All-time high is 84 by Fred Herd in 1898. The post-World War II high is 75 by Cary Middlecoff in 1949.

Youngest Champion — John J. McDermott was 19 years, 10 months and 14 days old when he won in 1911.

One last putt for the U.S. Open title.